Leisure & Community Services

Please return this item by the last date stamped below, to the library from which it was borrowed.

Renewals
You may renew any item twice (for 3 weeks) by telephone or post, providing it is not required by another reader. *Please quote the number stated below.*

Overdue charges
Please see library notices for the current rate of charges for overdue items. Overdue charges are not made on junior books unless borrowed on adult tickets.

Postage
Both adult and junior borrowers must pay any postage on overdue notices.

26 SEP 2003	2 2 SEP 2014	
1 6 MAR 2009		
1 5 DEC 2009		
- 9 SEP 2011		
2 6 NOV 2011		
- 5 MAR 2012		
2 5 APR 2012		
- 2 DEC 2013		

739.96

My War

ARP Volunteer

Stewart Ross

HODDER
Wayland

an imprint of Hodder Children's Books

Produced for Hodder Wayland by
Discovery Books Ltd
Unit 3, 37 Watling Street, Leintwardine, Shropshire SY7 0LW

First published in 2003 by Hodder Wayland, an imprint of Hodder Children's Books

British Library Cataloguing in Publication Data
Ross, Stewart
ARP volunteer. - (My war)
1. Air raid wardens - Great Britain - Juvenile literature
2. World War, 1939-1945 - War work - Great Britain - Juvenile literature
3. Great Britain - History - George VI, 1936-1952 - Juvenile literature
I. Title
940.5'316'0941

ISBN 0 7502 4215 9

Printed and bound by G. Canale & C. S.p.A. - Borgaro T.se - Italy

Series editor: Gianna Williams
Designer: Ian Winton
Picture research: Rachel Tisdale

Hodder Children's Books would like to thank the following for the loan of their material:
Corbis: pp. 6, 9 (bottom), 12, 13 (bottom), 16 (top and bottom), 17, 19; Hulton Archive: pp. 7, 10 (top),
11, 13 (top), 15, 18, 20, 22, 23, 24, 25 (top and bottom), 26, 27; RP Mitchell: p. 9 (top);
Robert Opie: pp. 8, 10 (bottom), 14, 21, 28, 29.
Cover: Hulton Archive (smaller picture), group photograph from personal collection of Donald Beerling.

Discovery Books would like to thank the following for the kind loan of their material:
Ted Ford, Laurie Goodwin, Doreen Hanks, Donald Beerling, Elsie Bewick, Helen Robertson,
Derek Butler and Pam Martin.

Hodder Children's Books
A division of Hodder Headline Limited
338 Euston Road
London NW1 3BH

Contents

ARP Volunteers

The Second World War (1939-45) was unlike any previous war. Experts feared bombers would destroy all Britain's large towns and cities. This did not happen. Even so, it was

TED FORD

Ted was born in Croydon, South London in 1926. He left school at 14 and worked in an instrument factory. From 1942-44 he was an ARP volunteer at his factory.

LAURIE GOODWIN

Laurie was 14 when war broke out in 1939. He remained at University College School, Hampstead, North London, and operated his own ARP stirrup pump team until 1945.

DOREEN HANKS

Doreen, a 27-year-old housewife, did ARP duties in the Oxfordshire village of Wendlebury, where she lived. Later, when her house filled with evacuees, she had to abandon ARP work.

a dangerous and terrifying time. The government set up a system of Air-Raid Precautions (ARP). Thousands of men and women volunteered for ARP work. This book tells the stories of six of them.

DONALD BEERLING

Thirteen when war broke out in 1941, Don joined the Civil Defence Messenger Service in his native Canterbury. He witnessed at first hand the Canterbury Blitz of 1942.

ELSIE BEWICK

Elsie (born 1915), from Durham, worked in her local branch of Woolworth's during the day. At night she served as an ARP worker on the shop roof.

HELEN ROBERTSON

Helen, who lived with her husband Jimmy in Clydebank, near Glasgow, worked as an air-raid warden throughout the war. She worked through the Clydebank Blitz of 13-14 March 1941.

This Country is at War

In September 1939 Nazi-controlled Germany invaded Poland. This led to Britain and France declaring war on Germany. The British people were not surprised – they had been expecting war with Germany for more than a year.

▲ The Nazi leader, Adolf Hitler, inspires his followers at a mass rally in 1938. Hitler aimed to expand his German empire into Eastern Europe.

ELSIE

We were having Sunday lunch when the news [of the outbreak of war] came – panic! We were all flying around trying to find shelter. It was very frightening.

TED

I was probably bewildered more than afraid, being only 13 years old. It wasn't until later we knew the devastation the constant bombing would or could do.

We had seen the newsreel shots of Manchuria [a Chinese province seized by the Japanese in 1931], Spain [where there was a civil war] and Abyssinia [modern Ethiopia, conquered by the Italians] and many people were quite terrified of air raids. Half the tenants of my father's flats fled to the countryside.

► Londoners are given their gas masks in case of an attack in September 1938.

The British government had been arranging its ARP services since 1936. It made sure every man, woman and child had been issued with a gas mask to protect against bombs of poisonous gas.

DON

I wasn't frightened but Poppy [Don's girlfriend whom he later married] was. There were so many horror stories – I couldn't believe I was in the same world as them. Some people said we were going to be invaded straight away and we had to set up barricades!

Thousands of air-raid shelters were built, too. For most people it was a dark and frightening time.

Everyone Needed

The Second World War was a 'total war'. This meant the countries involved used all their resources – industrial and agricultural as well as military – to bring about victory. The most important resource, of course, was the people.

ELSIE

All the shop staff were expected to do a shift – two or three nights a week – firewatching up on the roof. We had to keep an eye out for firebombs and put them out if any landed on the roof.

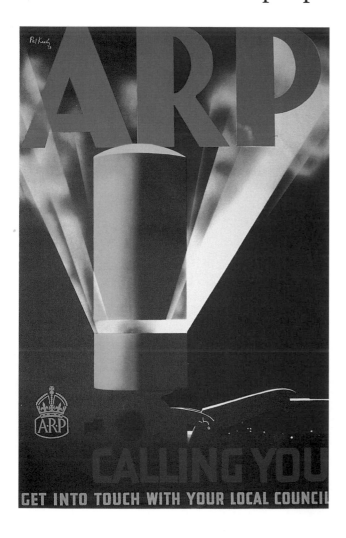

◀ A government poster, featuring a siren, calling on men and women to volunteer for much-needed ARP work.

LAURIE

Why did I become an ARP worker? One just did! No one thought about it much. We knew we had to do our bit. That's why I set up my stirrup pump team.

DON

I had been in the Scouts since before the war and the Scouts did war work automatically. I don't think we had much choice. I became an ARP messenger boy in 1941 – it was about the only ARP work a 14-year-old could do.

▼ Don among ARP colleagues in 1942. The building they are standing in front of was destroyed during an air raid the same year.

Millions of British men and women joined the armed forces. Others did important war service, working in factories that made weapons, for example. Large numbers of people also did voluntary work. The ARP service was run mostly by volunteers – some of whom had little choice about whether they did the work or not.

◀ Britain's ARP chief, Sir John Anderson, discusses recruitment with the leader of London County Council inside a mobile recruitment centre.

Getting Ready

The ARP services varied widely across the country. In large cities such as London, Birmingham, Manchester, Bristol and Glasgow the ARP was quite well organized. Most workers had uniforms (navy blue overalls) and were trained with the ambulance and fire services.

▲ On the lookout: women ARP volunteers in steel helmets on fire watch duty during the Blitz.

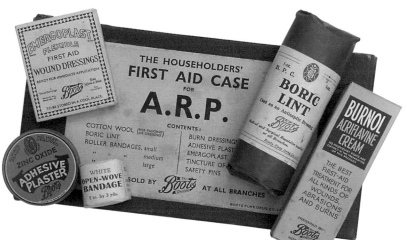

◄ Ready for anything – the first-aid kit issued to ARP workers. All ARP personnel received some first-aid training.

DOREEN

The base was my home – I was the only warden in the village! I don't know who was in charge of me.

I wore ordinary clothes with a tin hat. I carried a gas mask and an ID badge that showed who I was. Everyone knew, so there was not much point in it. I had a whistle, too.

DON

The clerk to Canterbury City Council was in charge of ARP. All the vehicles – fire engines and ambulances – were up on Chartham Downs, outside the city, so they wouldn't get hit.

The Messenger Service was in the Old Fish Market. The ARP centre was outside the municipal building, and the Rescue Service was in Orchard House, Wincheap. It was my job to go between them, especially if the phones went down. I was paid two-and-six [2 shillings and 6 pence, or 12p] a night.

I wore a boiler suit and a tin hat and carried a military-style gas mask, with a tube and a filter attached to the face mask.

In the smaller towns and villages it was often rather different. Here ARP workers frequently operated without either training or uniforms. Nevertheless, they always wore a white 'tin hat' (steel helmet) with 'ARP' or 'R' (Rescue) on it, and carried a gas mask.

◀ A uniformed boy scout acts as an ARP messenger on his bicycle.

Jacks of All Trades

The Air-Raid Precautions service carried out many different kinds of work. Before the war it distributed gas masks and leaflets on what to do in an air raid. It also planned where air-raid shelters and sirens were to go.

During the war ARP wardens had to see that the black-out was obeyed. When a raid was coming, the ARP service sounded warnings with sirens and whistles.

LAURIE

I was on firewatch duty once a month. Bombs were just bad luck if you got hit. I thought falling shrapnel from our own AA guns – splattering down like machine gun fire – was much more dangerous.

Wardens then directed people to the nearest air-raid shelter and made sure they were safe inside.

◀ An ARP warden tells Londoners where to go for help and refreshment after a night of bombing in 1941.

▲ An ARP warden keeps a look out during a Charlton v Arsenal football match in 1940.

▼ An ARP warden stops a taxi during an air-raid practice in June 1939.

Meanwhile, outside spotters and firewatchers kept an eye open for fire bombs. After a raid, ARP workers helped with rescue and keeping essential services going.

TED

We only became firewatchers, either during daylight air raids or throughout the night, as a duty. Rescue work became a natural task. In other words, you just got 'stuck in'. I assisted in the rescue of people from their bomb-torn homes – some from shelters, others hiding in cupboards under the stairs. We were not heroes or heroines, just doing what came naturally, saving your friends and neighbours. Tomorrow night it could be they who were digging you out.

Black-out

Any light visible from the air – especially street lights or lights from rows of houses – might help enemy bombers know where they were. This, in turn, would help them find their target. To prevent this happening, the government ordered a black-out.

TED

The black-out was routine in every household, whether at home or visiting friends. Any chink of light and wardens were shouting 'Put that light out!' or knocking on the offender's door.

Black-out regulations said that at night no lights were to be visible outside. All windows had to be covered with thick material; all public lights, including street lamps, were turned off; the lights on vehicles were reduced to thin beams.

▶ Advice to cyclists planning to travel during the black-out. As petrol was scarce during the war, the number of cyclists increased considerably.

LAURIE

I only bumped into anything once. But that was a lamp post – and it hurt!

LOOK OUT IN THE BLACK-OUT

REGULATION WHITE PATCH ON MUDGUARD

GOOD TYRES AND BRAKES

THE REAR LAMP MUST HAVE ONLY ONE APERTURE – NO BIGGER THAN A ONE-INCH CIRCLE THE LIGHT FROM WHICH MUST BE CLEARLY VISIBLE FROM 30 YDS BUT NOT VISIBLE AT 300 YDS

UPPER HALF OF FRONT LAMP GLASS AND WHOLE OF SIDE OR REAR PANELS MUST BE COMPLETELY OBSCURED; & LOWER HALF OF REFLECTOR MUST BE PAINTED WITH BLACK MATT PAINT OR OTHERWISE RENDERED INEFFECTIVE

NATIONAL SAFETY FIRST ASSOCIATION

Reg Gammon

Issued by THE NATIONAL "SAFETY FIRST" ASSOCIATION (Inc), Terminal House, 52, Grosvenor Gardens, London, S.W. 1
BLC/7.   PRINTED BY LOXLEY BROTHERS, LTD.

ARP wardens were responsible for seeing that the black-out was obeyed. For the first seven-and-a-half months of the war (September 1939-April 1940) air raids were rare. This made the wardens' task difficult – people believed the black-out was unnecessary. They soon changed their minds, however, when the serious raids began in the summer of 1940.

▲ A notice warning people of a black-out practice is posted in Paddington, London, in January 1939.

Sounding the Alarm

When enemy bombers crossed the Channel or the North Sea, they were picked up by radar or sighted by spotters. Warnings were then passed on to towns and cities that might be targets. Radar and spotters based inland gave a more accurate picture of where the enemy was headed.

▶ An ARP warden on a London rooftop during daylight. After September 1940 most raids came at night.

▲ Safe in an underground shelter, an ARP worker switches on his local air-raid siren. It was unusual for raiders to come as early as seven o'clock in the evening.

DOREEN

I had to blow my whistle when there was a raid coming. Where we lived, in the country, not many people could hear the siren. My whistle was the only warning. There was only one big air-raid shelter in Wendlebury, large enough for most people who wanted to get into it. I used to make buckets of cocoa for the people in the shelter.

When the bombers approached a target, a 'red warning' (danger) was given and the ARP services or police sounded the air-raid warning sirens. These were a warning to everyone to take cover. ARP wardens hurried people into shelters and made sure there were no lights showing. A few minutes later, the sound of the enemy aircraft could be heard in the distance.

ELSIE

The sirens went off most nights. They made an eerie droning noise. I find the sound frightening even today. There's a quarry nearby and when they're going to use explosives they let off a siren. It's exactly the same sound as during the war – and it's still frightening.

◄ All clear! An ARP warden in northern England signals with a bell that the enemy bombers have gone.

Taking Shelter

Broadly speaking, there were two types of air-raid shelter: purpose-built shelters and shelters converted from other uses.

Purpose-built shelters were of three types. The strongest were made of steel and concrete and set deep into the ground. Some of these shelters held hundreds of people. Anderson shelters, designed to hold one family, were made of sheets of curved steel. They were set up outside people's homes

▲ A family, all carrying their gas masks, enter the Anderson shelter in their garden.

and partly covered with earth. The Morrison shelter was a large metal table with wire mesh round the sides. It was placed inside the house. Those taking refuge in Morrison shelters were often trapped if their house collapsed around them.

DON

The Morrison was a death trap. If you were inside when your house got bombed you couldn't get out. Lots of people were burned to death in Morrison shelters.

The most common shelters converted from other uses were the London Underground stations. Hundreds of thousands of Londoners sheltered there every night. Other shelters included caves and tunnels, such as those under the cities of Nottingham and Liverpool.

▼ After a night in an underground shelter, Londoners set off to work the next morning.

HELEN

The entrances – called 'close mouths' – of tenement blocks were fortified to withstand blast. There were also shelters in the back courts. I remember they were freezing cold – people lit a candle in a flower pot to take the chill off.

Blitz!

The British adopted the German word 'Blitzkrieg' ('lightning war') and shortened it to 'Blitz'. They used it to mean a heavy bombing raid or series of raids.

Outside London, especially after 1941, raids were infrequent and ARP work was often dull and routine.

For about one year, however, from the summer of 1940, many British cities were heavily 'blitzed' – some many times. For several months London was raided almost daily.

◄ ARP workers search bomb-damaged shops and houses in the Holborn district of London in October 1940.

LAURIE

I was on top of Hampstead Heath the night they set London docks on fire. In those days there were no trees and you could see right down to the docks. The red glow covered the whole sky, as far as you could see, east and west. It made you think.

IF YOU ARE BOMBED OUT
and have no friends to go to

ask a
POLICEMAN
or your **WARDEN**
where to find your
REST CENTRE

ISSUED BY THE MINISTRY OF HEALTH

◄ A poster gives information to those whose homes have been destroyed. The rest centres were staffed by volunteers.

ELSIE

They did try to bomb the city of Durham once. I was with my parents in a shelter at the bottom of the garden when the bombers came overhead. At that moment a thick fog came over the cathedral and the city centre. The bombers couldn't see a thing and went away. They say it was a heavenly fog.

In 1942, after RAF raids on ancient German cities, the Luftwaffe (German air force) bombed historic cathedral cities, including Canterbury. These were called 'Baedecker Raids' because the targets had supposedly been selected from the Baedecker guide book.

DOREEN

My worst moment as an ARP warden was when they tried to bomb the airfield at Weston-on-the-Green. The bombs landed nearby and killed a whole field of cattle. It was a terrible mess.

21

Firewatchers

Three common types of bomb were landmines, high explosives (HE) and incendiaries (or 'firebombs'). Landmines were designed to explode at ground level, causing the maximum damage to buildings. HE bombs ploughed into the ground before exploding, leaving a large crater. Incendiary bombs were the most common. They were small cylinders (about 40-50 cm long and 10 cm in diameter) containing a flammable substance (such as magnesium) that burst into flames on landing.

▶ A bomb crater in the centre of the Strand, London, in September 1940.

ARP firewatchers, often sitting on roofs, tried to spot where incendiaries fell and cover them with sand before they caught fire. Stirrup pump teams used buckets of water and hand-operated pumps to quench fires before they took hold.

Obviously firewatching could be described as dangerous when we were on duty during a raid; once the fires had taken hold the aircraft had a target to aim at. That made it worse.

▶ A stirrup pump team dashes through the deserted streets to the scene of a fire.

HELEN

I remember huge bombs called 'landmines' floating down on parachutes. They actually looked beautiful in the moonlight. Incendiary bombs were like flowers on a carpet when they went off.

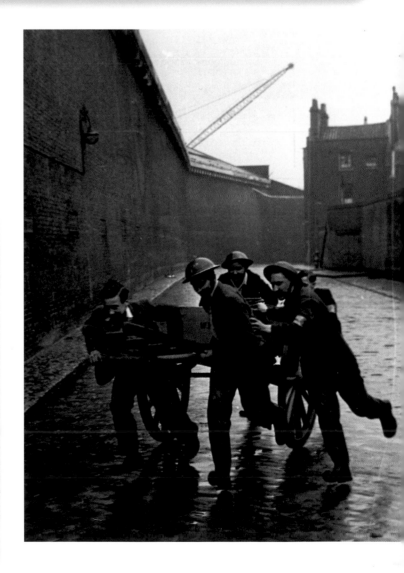

Difficult Times

Many ARP workers remember the friendship and comradeship of the war years, when everyone was pulling together. People had fun, too.

Nevertheless, enemy bombing killed over 60,000 civilians during the war and destroyed over 2 million homes.

▲ Although a bomb had destroyed her home, little Barbara James was safely carried out by this ARP warden in June 1940.

At some time or another, therefore, most ARP workers came face to face with the horrors of war: death, horrible injuries, suffering and misery.

TED

I helped with rescue work on many occasions: helping with stretchers, digging people out, that sort of thing. There was always someone around who would organize you into a team. I don't think we always knew who that person was.

◀ Carefully does it: rescue workers lift an injured man from a blitzed house.

▼ An ARP worker comes to the aid of an injured soldier near a hospital in May 1940.

DON

I spent the morning cleaning windows in Sturry, near Canterbury. Sixpence [two new pence] a house I charged. I knew all the people. Later that day a landmine landed on Sturry station. There were the same people, the ones whose windows I had cleaned and had paid me their sixpences, coming out on stretchers. Wounded and dead. ARP people did a first-aid course with St John's Ambulance, so I lent a hand. The same people. I'll never forget it.

Victory

There were few bombing raids over Britain by 1944. In June that year, however, the Germans started sending over missiles. First came V-1s, which were like jet bombers with no pilots. In September the first V-2s hit Britain. They were supersonic missiles with one tonne of high explosive in the nose. Together the V-1s and V-2s caused about 54,000 casualties.

DON

Lots of 'Doodle-bugs' – that's what the V-1s were called because of the noise they made, whirring – went overhead. You knew when they were going to come down because the engine cut out. They were aimed at London but most fell in Kent. All over the place.

There was almost nothing ARP staff could do about the missile attacks, except help with the wounded and clear the wreckage afterwards.

◀ A German V-2 flying bomb on its launcher, 1945. Flying faster than the speed of sound, it could not be shot down.

Nevertheless, V-1 and V-2 attacks proved to be a final fling by a defeated enemy. Invaded on all sides by Allied troops, the Nazis finally surrendered on 7 May, 1945 – Victory in Europe (VE) Day.

ELSIE

When VE Day came we went straight to the nearest church to remember the dead and give thanks that it was all over. At last. It was a very traumatic experience.

TED

In 1944 I was called up into the army and so stopped doing ARP work. I have no recollection whether I was glad to stop or not – war is war.

◀ A celebratory children's tea party at war's end in 1945.

Looking Back

The ARP was disbanded when the war in Europe ended in May 1945. As most ARP workers were volunteers, they simply returned to full-time civilian life.

DOREEN

I was glad when I stopped being a warden but pleased I did it. It was quite an experience!

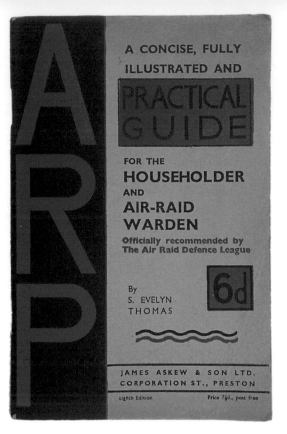

▲ All you need to know for sixpence! Guides like this one were sold in large numbers before the war, when people did not know what an air raid would be like.

All the ARP workers in this book looked back on their wartime experience with mixed feelings. They would never want the killing, suffering and destruction to return. Nevertheless, they all feel that there was something special about the war – a spirit of comradeship, of being part of the same united team – that can never be recaptured.

TED

I continued as an infantry soldier until 1948, serving in Palestine and Egypt. Occasionally you look back at the good and bad times of those years, remembering your friends.

LAURIE

The borough organized a stirrup pump team competition at the end of the war – find an incendiary bomb (pretend) and put it out. My team – myself (aged 18), my younger sister and a woman of 22 – came first but they put us second because we weren't adults.

▶ Laurie (standing) and his younger sister (sitting far right) were too young to win the stirrup pump competition.

▲ A card game invented for people to play during the long hours they had to spend indoors during the black-out.

DON

War brings out the best and worst in people. A lot of good came out of it: the comradeship, the realization that people are more important than things.

Glossary

AA anti-aircraft.

Anderson shelter air-raid shelter made of semi-circles of corrugated steel.

Armed forces army, navy and air force.

ARP Air-Raid Precautions.

Baffle wall an external wall built across the entrance of a house to stop light showing during a black-out.

Black-out regulations stating that no light was to be visible outside at night time.

Blast force of an explosion.

Blitz heavy bombing attack (from the German word 'Blitzkrieg').

Civil Defence forces and organization for defending Britain.

Civilians not members of the armed forces.

Corrugated moulded into ripples.

Evacuee someone who moved from a town or city to the countryside to escape the bombing.

Firewatching watching out for incendiary bombs and the fires they started.

Flammable burning easily.

HE high explosive.

ID identity.

Incendiary bomb bomb that burst into flames on landing.

Landmine high explosive bomb that was dropped by a parachute.

Morrison shelter an indoor air-raid shelter. It was a steel table with mesh round the sides.

Nazi German National Socialist Party led by Adolf Hitler.

Radar short for Radio Detection and Ranging. A way of spotting metal objects from far away by bouncing radio waves off them.

RAF short for Royal Air Force.

Stirrup pump hand-operated pump with a loop (stirrup) at the bottom so the operator could hold it steady with their foot.

Tenant someone who pays rent for a flat or house.

Tenement large block of flats.

V-1 early German missile, like a pilotless jet aircraft.

V-2 later German missile that flew faster than the speed of sound.

VE Day Victory in Europe Day, 8 May 1945.

Further Reading

Non-fiction

Gardner, Faye, *In Grandma's Day: Grandma's War*, Evans, 2000.

Langley, Andrew, *The Blitz*, Heinemann, 1995.

Parsons, Martin, *The History Detective Investigates United Kingdom at War: Air Raids*, Hodder Wayland, 1999.

Reynoldson, Fiona, *The Home Front: The Blitz*, Hodder Wayland, 1993.

Robson, Pam, *All About the Second World War*, Hodder Wayland, 1996.

Ross, Stewart, *At Home in World War II, the Blitz*, Evans, 2002.

Fiction

Ross, Stewart, *Dear Mum, I Miss You!*, Evans, 2001.

Ross, Stewart, *What If the Bomb Goes Off?*, Evans, 2001.

Westall, Robert, *Blitz*, Collins, 1995.

Westall, Robert, *Cascades: Blitz*, Collins, 2001.

Resources

Places to Visit

Museum of London.

Battle of Britain Museum, Hawkinge, Kent.

'Hellfire Corner', Dover Castle.

Coventry Cathedral, where ruins of the original cathedral destroyed in air raids during the Second World War were incorporated into the new building.

Index

Numbers in *italics* indicate photographs.